hide
this
spanish
book
for lovers

Berlitz Publishing
New York   Munich   Singapore

Hide This Spanish Book for Lovers

Contacting the Editors
Every effort has been made to provide accurate information in this publication, but changes are inevitable. The publisher cannot be responsible for any resulting loss, inconvenience or injury. We would appreciate it if readers would call our attention to any errors or outdated information by contacting Berlitz Publishing, 193 Morris Avenue, Springfield, NJ 07081, USA. email: comments@berlitzbooks.com

First Printing: Spring 2006
Printed in China

ISBN 981-246-848-X

Writer: Isabel Mendoza, Noël Baca Castex
Editorial Director: Sheryl Olinsky Borg
Senior Editor/Project Manager: Lorraine Sova
Assistant Editor: Emily Bernath
Production Manager: Elizabeth Gaynor
Cover and Interior Design: Blair Swick, Wee Design Group
Illustrations: Kyle Webster, Amy Zaleski

Hide This Spanish Book for lovers has everything from pick-up lines to erotic sex talk. "Hot" words are labeled with 🌡 and the hottest language with 🌡. Go ahead— get hot 'n heavy with Spanish.

table of contents

¿Vienes aquí seguido?

<u>beeyeh</u>-nehs ah<u>kee</u> seh<u>gee</u>do

hooking up

4

Come here often?

It sounds better in Spanish.

hooking up

¿Estás solo♂?

ehstahs solo

¿Estás so♀la?

ehstahs solah

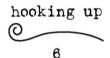

hooking up

8

Are you alone?

*Make sure that guy or girl
you're after isn't taken.*

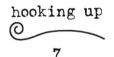

hooking up

¿Quieres tomar algo?

keeyeh-rehs tomahr ahlgo

hooking up

8

Can I buy you a drink?

A typical line—but it works everytime.

¿Bailamos?

buy<u>lah</u>mos

hooking up

10

Wanna dance?

An ideal way to get close to someone.

¿Puedo llevarte a tu casa?

pwehdo yehbahrteh ah too kahsah

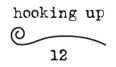

hooking up

12

Can I take
you home?

Get some alone time.

hooking up

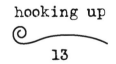

13

hooking up

14

the scoop

Latinos are very "machistas" although—fortunately—this attitude is changing. However, in almost all Spanish-speaking countries, the man approaches the woman. A girl who dares to make the first move is very often taken for a tease or even a slut! In spite of this, a girl can pick up a guy she likes, with a little imagination. An ordinary question, "¿Tienes hora?" (What time is it?) can be a way to get a guy's attention. A woman who knows what she wants can also use her eyes—without being too provocative—to attract interest.

hooking up

¡Qué papito!

keh pah<u>pee</u>to

¡Qué mamita!

keh mah<u>mee</u>tah

hooking up

16

What a hottie!

Literally: What a daddy!
What a mommy!

Está guapísimo.

ehstah gwahpeesee-mo

Está guapísima.

ehstah gwahpeesee-mah

He is very cute.

She is very cute.

They would make the perfect pair.

¡Está divino!

ehs<u>tah</u> dee<u>bee</u>no

¡Está divina!

ehs<u>tah</u> dee<u>bee</u>nah

He is divine!

She is divine!

Just heavenly, right?!

Esa mujer es toda una hembrota.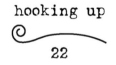

ehsah moo<u>khehr</u> ehs <u>to</u>dah <u>oo</u>nah ehm<u>bro</u>tah

She's a totally hot woman.

Literally: That woman is a total female.

Guys, you can say this to your buddies but don't say it to a lady—it's offensive!

hooking up

¡Tremendo bizcocho!

trehmehndo beeskocho

¡Tremendo bombón!

trehmehndo bombon

hooking up

Totally cute!

Literally: Tremendous cupcake!
Tremendous bonbon!

The diminutive "bizcochito" and
"bomboncito" are also terms of
endearment.

hooking up

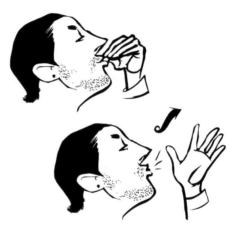

hooking up

Butter up a potential date with flattery! It's common in Spanish to compliment someone by comparing him or her to something tasty— a bonbon, a cupcake, or "dulce", a sweet, etc. If you see a cutie walking down the street, go ahead and let him or her know how delicious he or she is by "kissing" your fingers and saying "ummmm", *mmm*, to reinforce your pleasure.

Bésame.

behsahmeh

kisses & hugs

Kiss me.

Ah, instant gratification...

kisses & hugs

Dame un beso.

dahmeh oon behso

kisses & hugs

30

Give me a kiss.

Be demanding!

kisses & hugs

Acaríciame…

ahkah<u>ree</u>-seeyahmeh

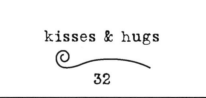

kisses & hugs

32

Caress me...

Need some physical attention?

kisses & hugs

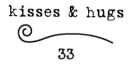

33

Estoy caliente.

ehs<u>toy</u> kah<u>leeyehn</u>-teh

I'm horny.

Literally: I'm hot.

kisses & hugs

35

¿Es eso la marca de un chupón?

ehs <u>ehso</u> lah <u>mahr</u>kah deh oon choo<u>pon</u>

kisses & hugs

36

Is that a hickey?

Thought you could cover it up, huh?!

kisses & hugs

Hazme el *amor*.

ahsmeh ehl ahmor

kisses & hugs

38

Make *love* to me.

A romantic way to say it.

kisses & hugs

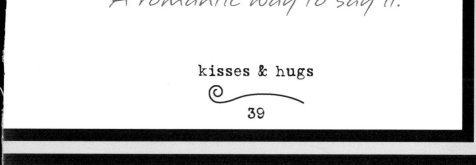

kisses & hugs

40

the scoop

Latinos are very affectionate people. They not only use an impressive array of words and phrases to express love, but they like touching, hugging, kissing, and all kinds of physical affection, even with people they've just met. If you find yourself in Latin America, don't be surprised to get some extra lovin'. Lucky you!

kisses & hugs

Sólo estamos vacilando.

solo eh<u>sta</u>hmos bahsee<u>lahn</u>-doh

kisses & hugs

We're just fooling around.

Meaning: NOT monogamous!

kisses & hugs

Somos amigovios.

somos ahmee<u>go</u>-beeyos

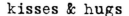
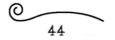

We're friends with benefits.

Literally: We're a pseudo-couple.

Enjoy sex—without the commitment!

kisses & hugs

45

Estamos saliendo.

ehs<u>tah</u>mos sah<u>leeyehn</u>-doh

kisses & hugs

We're dating.

Serious stuff, huh?

Él es mi novio.
ehl ehs mee nobeeyo
Ella es mi novia.
eh-yah ehs mee nobeeyah

He's my boyfriend.

She's my girlfriend.

Let everyone know!

kisses & hugs

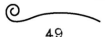

 **Somos** *amantes.*

somos ahmahntehs

kisses & hugs

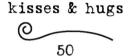

50

 **We're** *lovers.*

With all the fringe benefits...

kisses & hugs

51

Estamos enamoradísimos.

ehs<u>tah</u>mos ehnahmorah-<u>dee</u>seemos

kisses & hugs

We are very much in *love.*

First comes love, then comes...

kisses & hugs

53

¿Quieres "divertirte"?

keeyeh-rehs deebehrteer-teh

love & sex

Do you wanna "party"?

...All night long?!

love & sex

55

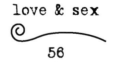

¡Quiero comerte a besos!

<u>keeyeh</u>-ro ko<u>mehr</u>teh ah <u>beh</u>sos

love & sex

56

I could just eat you up!

He or she is just delicious, huh?!

love & sex

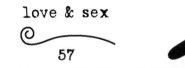

Vayamos a la habitación.

bah<u>yah</u>mos ah lah ahbeetah-<u>seeyon</u>

love & sex

Let's go to the bedroom.

You're not tired, are you?!

love & sex

59

¿Puedo hacerte masajes?

pwehdo ahsehrteh mahsahkhehs

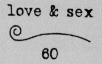

love & sex

60

Can I give you a massage?

Foot, neck, back... take your pick!

Te deseo.

teh deh<u>seho</u>

love & sex

love & sex

Sácate la ropa.

sahkahteh lah ropah

Take off your clothes.

love & sex

65

Hagámoslo.

ahg<u>ah</u>moslo

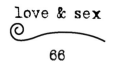

love & sex

Let's have sex.

No foolin' around...

Dime cochinadas.

<u>dee</u>meh kochee<u>nah</u>dahs

Talk dirty to me.

Whatever puts you in the mood.

love & sex

69

Usémos la imaginación.

oo<u>seh</u>mos lah eemahkheenah-<u>seeyon</u>

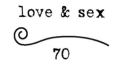

love & sex

70

Let's get kinky.

Literally: Let's use our imagination.

Latinos may be subtle with their words but not in their actions.

love & sex

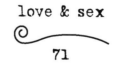

71

love & sex

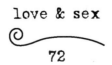

the Scoop

There's a reason why Latin passion is such an infamous phrase. Maybe it's got something to do with the sultry climate or spicy foods, but Latinos are known for being sex gods and goddesses. Intense in and out of the bedroom, most Latinos aren't afraid to express their passions—verbally or physically!

love & sex

¿Dónde está mi vibrador?

dondeh ehstah mee beebrahdor

love & sex

Where's my vibrator?

Toys are fun.

Ponte ropa interior sexy.

ponteh ropah eenteh-reeyor sehksee

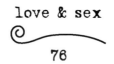

love & sex

76

Put on some erotic underwear.

¿Quieres ver una porno?

keeyeh-rehs behr oonah porno

Wanna watch a porno?

*You need to do something
to pass the time!*

love & sex

¿Tienes condones?

<u>teeyeh</u>-nehs kon<u>do</u>nehs

love & sex

80

Do you have condoms?

That's a forward question, isn't it?

Usemos un condón
con sabor.

oo<u>se</u>hmos oon kon<u>don</u> kon sah<u>bor</u>

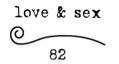

love & sex

Let's use
a flavored condom.

Cherry, chocolate, or coconut?

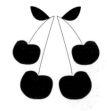

Tócame.

tokahmeh

love & sex

84

Touch me.

Go ahead...

love & sex

85

¿Te gusta?

teh <u>goos</u>tah

love & sex

★ ★ ★ ★ ★ ★ ★ ★ ★

Does that feel good?

Sure does...

★ ★ ★ ★ ★ ★ ★ ★ ★

love & sex

¿Tienes alguna fantasía sexual?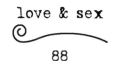

teeyeh-nehs ahlgoonah fahntah-seeah sehkswahl

love & sex

88

Do you have any sexual fantasies?

What do you have in mind?

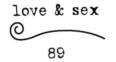

love & sex

89

Tuvimos sexo.

tou<u>bee</u>mos <u>seh</u>kso

love & sex

90

We had sex.

Simple and straightforward.

love & sex

91

Dormimos juntos.

dormeemos khoontos

We slept together.

Did you actually get some sleep?
Hope not!

love & sex

93

♥
Pasamos la noche.

pah<u>sah</u>mos lah <u>no</u>cheh

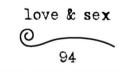

We spent the night together.

Lucky you!

love & sex

Te quiero.

teh <u>keeyeh</u>-ro

I *love* you.

Another option is "te amo"
but save it for someone you're
head over heels for!

u + me 4ever

Me gusta como me haces el *amor.*

meh <u>goo</u>stah <u>ko</u>mo meh <u>ah</u>sehs ehl ah<u>mor</u>

u + me 4ever

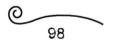

98

I like the way you make *love* to me.

Give him or her an ego boost.

u + me 4ever

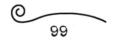

99

¡Eres bueno♂!

ehrehs bwehno

¡Eres buena!♀

ehrehs bwehnah

You're good (in bed)!

Thanks for the compliment.

Lo pase muy bien (anoche).

lo pah<u>seh</u> mwee beeyehn (ah<u>no</u>cheh)

u + me 4ever

I had a great time with you (last night).

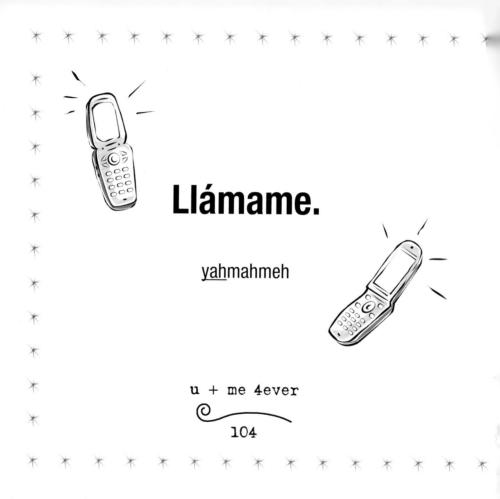

Llámame.

yahmahmeh

u + me 4ever

104

Call me.

Cross your fingers that

he or she does...

u + me 4ever

¿Puedo verte de nuevo?

<u>pweh</u>do <u>behr</u>teh deh <u>nweh</u>bo

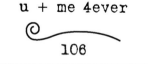

No puedo vivir sin ti.

no <u>pweh</u>do bee<u>beer</u> seen tee

u + me 4ever

108

I can't live without you.

You're obsessed!

u + me 4ever

109

Vente a vivir conmigo.

behnteh ah beebeer konmeego

u + me 4ever

110

Move in with me.

Pack your bags and go!

Cásate conmigo.

<u>kah</u>sahteh kon<u>mee</u>ego

u + me 4ever

112

Marry me.

Where's the ring?!

u + me 4ever
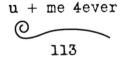
113

Estoy embarazada.

ehs<u>toy</u> ehmbahrah-<u>sah</u>dah

u + me 4ever

114

I'm pregnant.

Mental note: "embarazada" doesn't mean "embarrassed"!

mi amor

mee ah<u>mor</u>

mi amorcito

mee ahmor<u>see</u>to

my love

my little love

The diminutive form makes everything a little cuter.

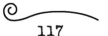

sweet talk

bebé

behbeh

cariño

kahreenyo

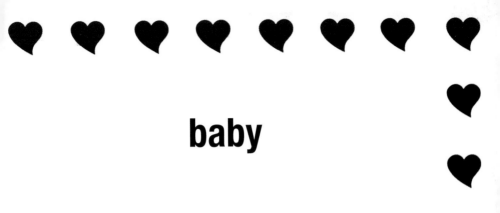

baby

darling

For the sweetheart in your life...

papi / papit♂

pahpee / pahpeeto

mami / mamita♀

mahmee / mahmeetah

honey

Literally: daddy / mommy

Who's your daddy?

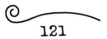

terroncito de azúcar

tehrron<u>see</u>to deh ah<u>soo</u>kahr

sweet talk

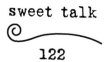

122

sugar

Literally: sugar cube

sweet talk

123

sweet talk
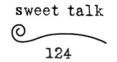
124

the scoop

The most well-known Spanish term of endearment is "cielito lindo"; it literally means little pretty sky. The phrase was immortalized by a popular Mexican mariachi song. You don't have to be in a mariachi band to share this pet name with your lover! Go ahead and give it a try.

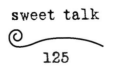

Seamos sólo amigos.

sehahmos solo ahmeegos

Let's just be friends.

A classy way to end it.

breaking up

127

the end

128